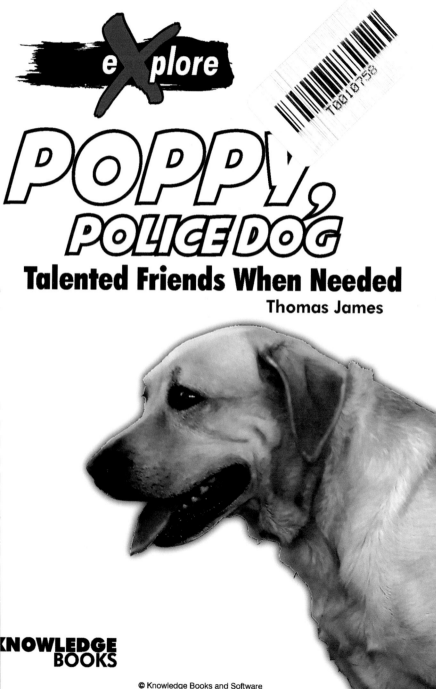

eXplore

POPPY, POLICE DOG
Talented Friends When Needed

Thomas James

KNOWLEDGE
BOOKS

© Knowledge Books and Software

Teacher Notes:

Meet Poppy, the friendly and very intelligent Labrador who started off life with a very important job. Join the author as he recounts Poppy's life sniffing out drugs for the Police Drug Squad. Learn about why he retired and how other Labradors like Poppy have become very important and helpful members of our society. No wonder we call them man's best friend!

Discussion points for consideration:

1. What other dog breeds are helpful to humans and why?

2. What breed of dog is your favorite and why?

3. Talk about the importance of being a responsible pet owner.

Difficult words to be introduced and practiced before reading this book:

Labrador, retrieving, popular, dangerous, intelligent, vision, squad, underwater, rewarded, distances, cupboards, normal, retired, muzzle, naughty, neighbors, raisin, hospital, recovered, poisonous, digest, carnivores, fortnight.

Contents

1. Who is Poppy and Where Did He Come From?

Poppy is a big, happy, and friendly Labrador. Labradors are a breed of dog.

The Labrador breed started in Newfoundland and Labrador, Canada.

Labradors were used for hunting and retrieving. The dogs would jump into the icy waters to retrieve ducks and seals. The dogs could handle the cold water and ice. They also loved to swim.

2. The Labrador Dog Breed

Labradors are a very popular dog across the world. Why are they popular? There are many reasons that people love Labradors. Here are some:

- Labradors are a medium-sized dog.

- They play happily with children.

- They are not dangerous to people or other animals.

- They are very intelligent and easy to train.

- They are very loving and playful.

- They are not fussy eaters.

- They are easy to care for.

Is a Labrador the best dog for you? There are many reasons to love Labradors. You also need to think of these things before getting one:

- Labradors are big eaters and can get very fat.

- Some Labradors can have pain with their hips.

- They can shed a lot of hair when it gets warm.

- Labradors get lonely quickly.

- Some will bark all night if upset.

- Labradors can make a lot of mess when playing.

3. Labradors as Guide Dogs

Labradors are smart dogs. They are very friendly. They are the perfect dog to train for many jobs.

Some Labradors are trained to be guide dogs for people with low vision. Guide dogs are seeing eye dogs. They must keep calm and be willing to work for their owner.

9

There was once a lady with a calm and very smart Labrador. It was the perfect Labrador for her. She loved it with all her heart.

The Labrador would guide her to her work in the city. It would wait at the crossing until the cars stopped and the walk sign came on. The Labrador always walked so the woman could keep pace.

The Labrador had one small weakness. On their morning walk to her office, the woman noticed a stop that did not seem right.

The dog would take a short cut through a bakery and stop at the cake window. Every morning, the bakery owner would allow the dog to point to the yummy cake it wanted to eat.

4. Poppy's Job with the Police

Poppy was bought by the Police Drug Squad when he was a puppy. He was trained to sniff out drugs. He went to prisons, airports, wharves, and houses. Poppy had no time to play and be silly.

Poppy was very good at his job. He was trained to find drugs in different places. He sometimes swam underwater to find drugs thrown from boats. He found drugs hidden in walls and under beds.

Poppy barked to let his trainer know when he had found drugs. The trainer made it like a game for Poppy. When Poppy found the drugs, he was rewarded with food and a toy. Dogs like Poppy can smell things over long distances.

17

Poppy had a problem as he got older – he got too big to fit under beds.

He grew too big to sniff into small cupboards for drugs. One day he got stuck in a bag room on a plane.

Poppy grew and grew and weighed over 128 pounds. He wasn't fat but just a very big dog. Sadly, he had to retire at 3 years old.

Why did Poppy grow nearly twice as big as his brothers and sisters? His father, Chico, was a big dog but not twice as big! His mother Holly was a normal size Labrador.

Poppy was born the same size as the other pups. He just grew much bigger. He was the only big dog from that litter. It seems that some genes switched on and made Poppy grow very big.

5. Poppy's New Life and Friends

Poppy now loves to play with his friends at the dog park. He has retired from working with the Police.

Poppy loves to swim. He loves looking for little fish in the water. He also loves to walk through the mud and comes home with muddy feet.

Poppy is twice as big as a normal Labrador. However, Poppy thinks he is a little dog.

He loves running and playing with other dogs and children. Maybe he thinks he is a little dog and not a very big Labrador!

Poppy wears a muzzle as he is strong and will pull his owner to where he wants to go. When Poppy is taken to the dog park he meets up with his friends and has lots of games.

6. Poppy Loves Eating!

Poppy is very naughty when he wants to be. He loves eating. Most Labradors love eating!

He often tricks his owners into thinking he has not been fed and gets an extra meal. Poppy also visits the neighbors and smiles and wags his tail. He stands next to their fridge, hoping to be fed.

When Poppy travels in the car, he sits in his doggy seat. He smells many smells that humans can't smell. When he goes past take away food places, he licks his lips and howls as he wants the cooked chicken. He is very funny to watch!

Dogs have a strong sense of smell. Humans can smell well, but a dog's sense of smell is 1,000 times better! Dogs have often been used as trackers by police for search and rescue teams.

7. Dangerous Food for Dogs

One day Poppy ate something that nearly made him die. It came from a bag that fell out of the rubbish. What was the smallest thing that Poppy ate that could kill him? A raisin.

Poppy ate lots of raisins which are dried grapes. He quickly started to feel ill and was being sick. He was very weak and started to vomit.

We took Poppy to the vet straight away. He had to stay in hospital until he recovered. Now we are very careful about what Poppy eats.

Grapes, raisins, and currants are all poisonous to dogs. They can kill a dog if they are not treated. Poppy was lucky that he was only in hospital for three days.

Chocolate is also very dangerous for dogs. It works like a poison on all dogs. They cannot digest it. It is important to give dogs the correct food.

Dogs are carnivores. This means they eat meat. Poppy can eat cooked chicken, turkey, beef, and fish. He also eats eggs, pumpkin, carrots, and spinach.

8. Poppy's Tricks and Helpful Ways

At night, Poppy sleeps in the laundry.
He has his own bed. However, he
loves to sneak inside at night.

Sometimes when everyone is asleep,
he will sneak in and sleep on the
couch. If he hears anyone coming
down the stairs, he quickly hops off.
He knows he is not supposed to sleep
there! You can always tell if he has
been sleeping there because there is
a warm spot.

Every second Friday, Poppy waits by the gate. He waits for the man driving the rubbish truck. Why would Poppy wait for the rubbish truck?

Every fortnight, the rubbish truck driver stops his truck and gives Poppy a treat. How does Poppy know that it is two weeks since the last visit? Do you think he can hear or smell the rubbish truck coming?

39

Poppy is a good watchdog. He barks when he hears noises outside the house.

He barks at snakes and possums as well. Dogs can hear four times further away than we can. They can hear noises like a snake sliding along or a possum climbing.

There was once a six-foot-long snake sleeping in the garage. Poppy started barking at the garage door. We lifted the door to see why he was barking. The snake fell on the man who opened the garage door. Poppy knew it was there!

One day a duck escaped the duck pen and went swimming in the river. Poppy's owner paddled down to try and bring the duck home.

Poppy decided to be helpful, and he jumped into the river. He swam towards the duck and guided it back to the house. Do you have a pet that is helpful like Poppy?

Word Bank

Labrador

retrieving

popular

dangerous

intelligent

vision

squad

underwater

rewarded

distances

cupboards

normal

retired

muzzle

naughty

neighbors

raisin

hospital

recovered

poisonous

digest

carnivores

fortnight